HOW TO DRAW CATS

You are talented. Enjoy!!!

INTRODUCTION

Cats are one of the most popular pets around the world, and they are incredibly smart creatures. With their bright eyes, perky ears, and playful tails, cats make wonderful subjects for drawing. Whether you are a cat person or a dog person, there is so much that you can learn by drawing a cat, including proportions, perspective, and fur detailing. All you need is to practice and not be afraid of making 'mistakes'. In this tutorial, we show you how to draw beautiful cats from different angles. If you are ready to learn how to draw a cat, then gather your supplies, get comfortable, and go for it!. I know you are an artist.

Just enjoy!

Felicity Burt

Don't be afraid to FAIL. Be afraid not to TRY.!!!

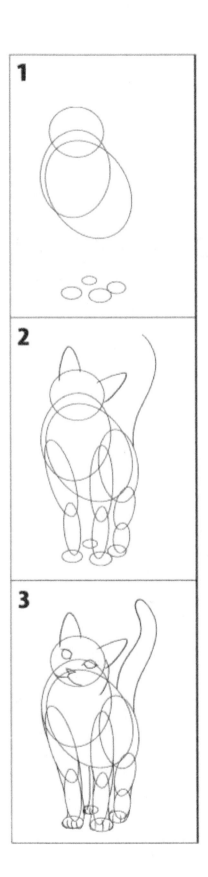

Your turn

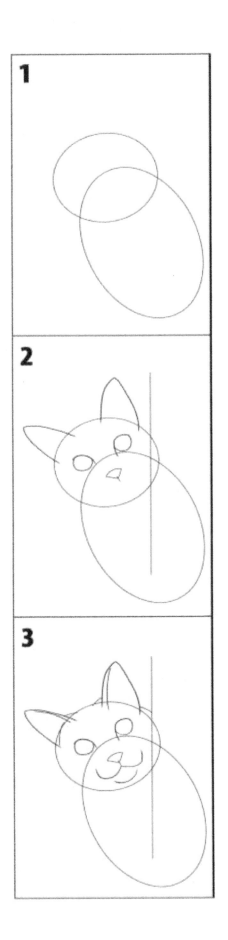

4

Your turn

4

Your turn

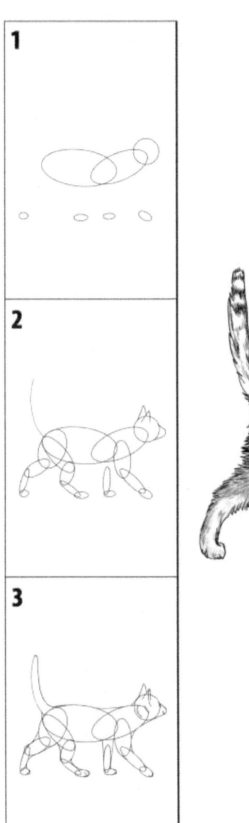

Your turn

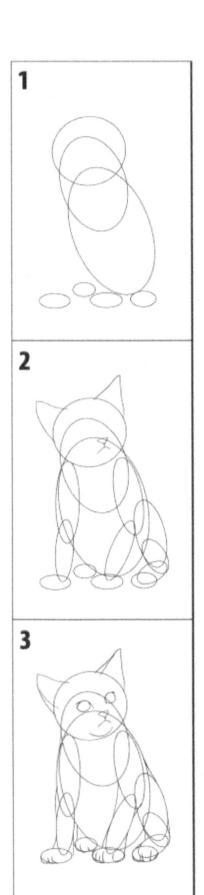

4

Your turn

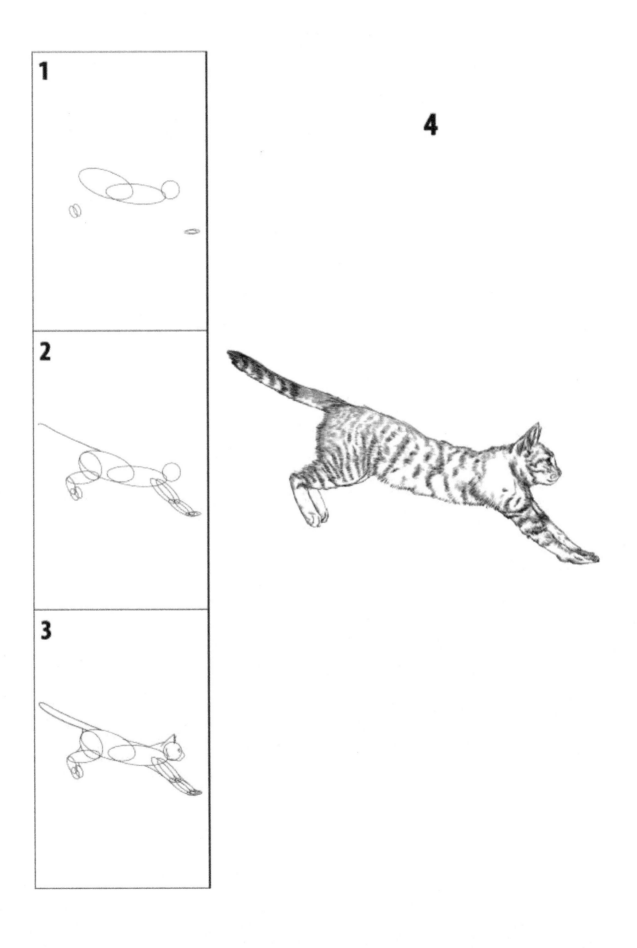

Your turn

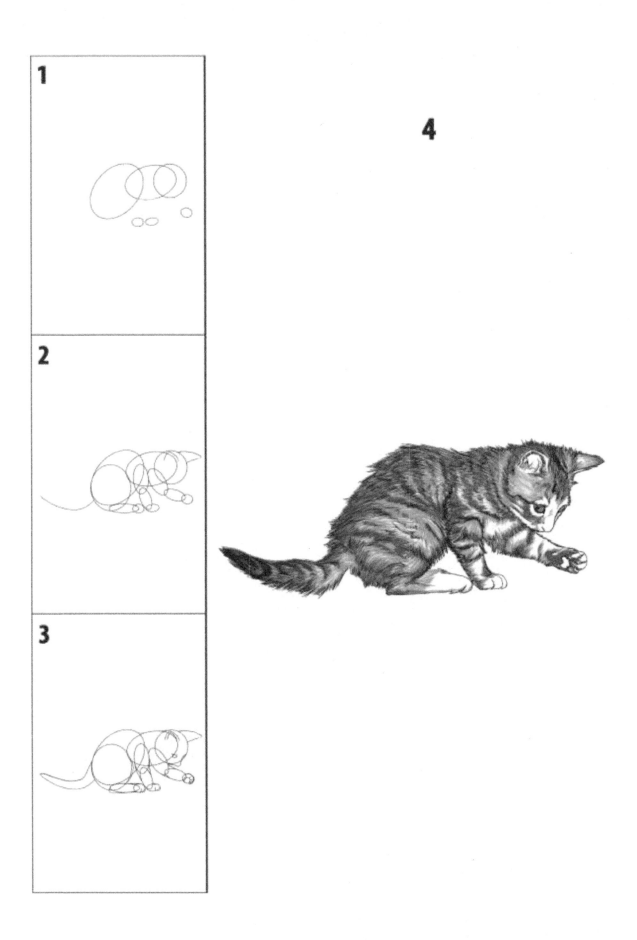

Your turn

1

2

3

4

Your turn

1

2

3

4

Your turn

Your turn

1

2

3

4

Your turn

4

Your turn

Your turn

1

2

3

4

Your turn

Your turn

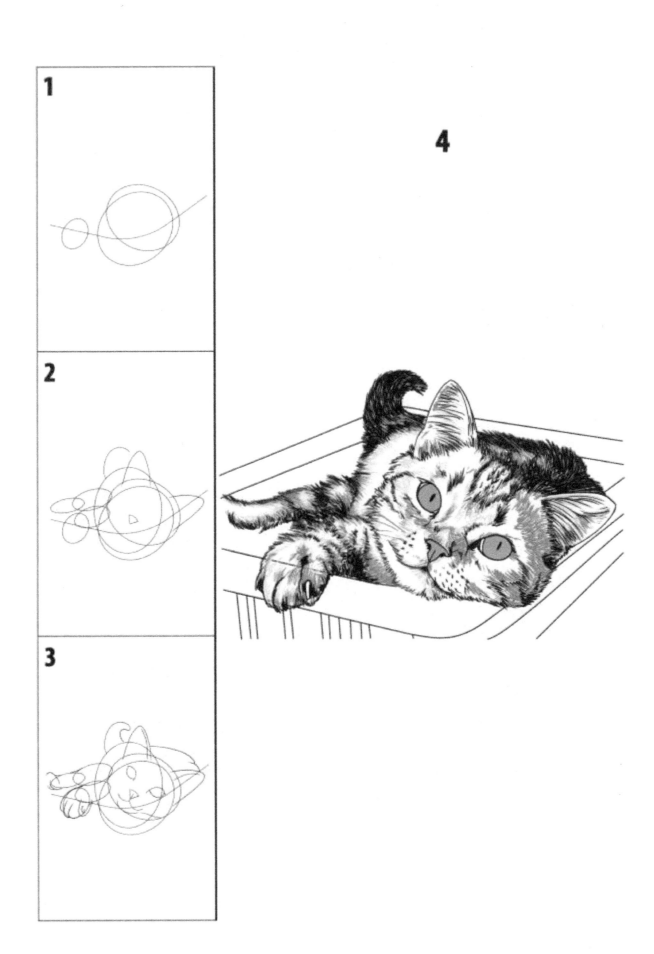

Your turn

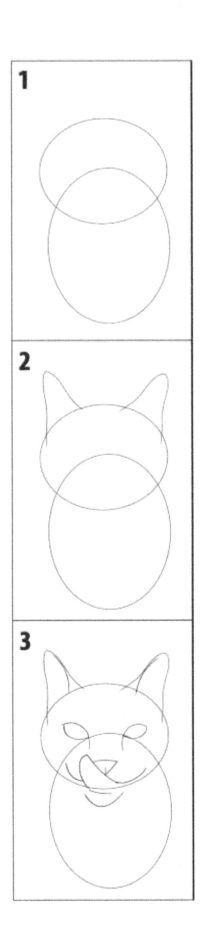

1

2

3

4

Your turn

4

Your turn

1

2

3

4

Your turn

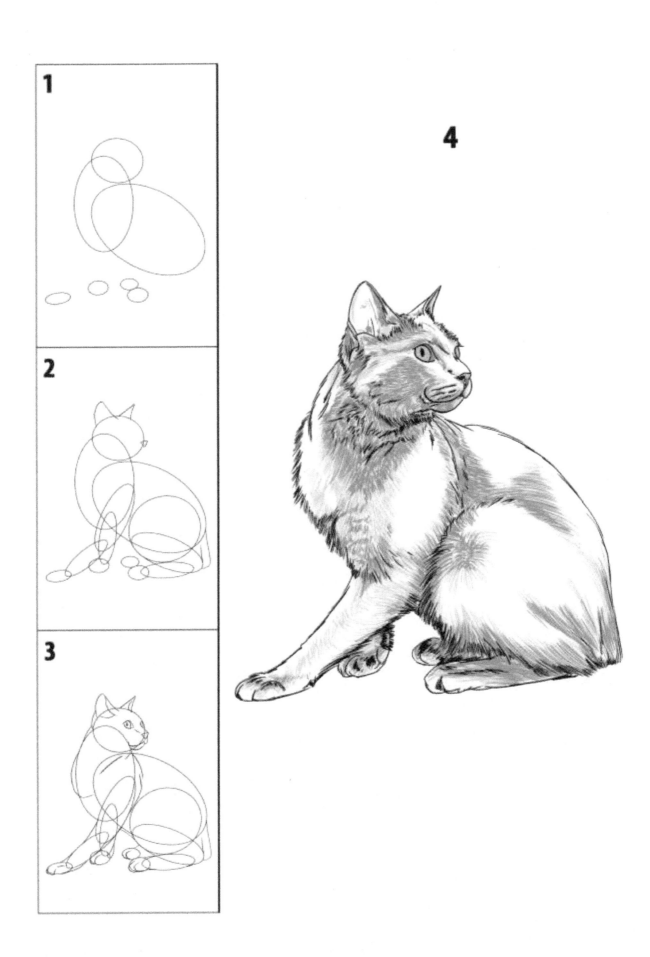

Your turn

1

2

3

4

Your turn

1

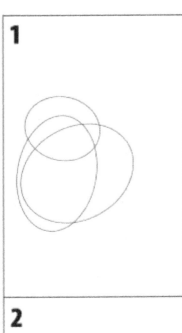

2

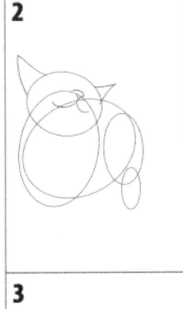

3

4

Your turn

1

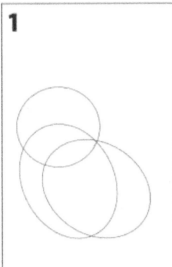

2

3

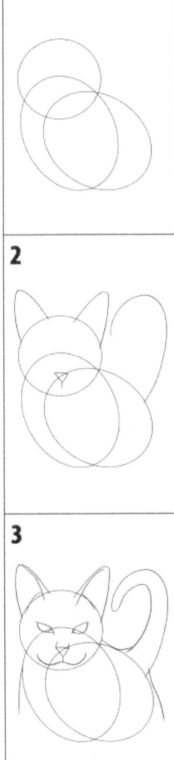

4

Your turn

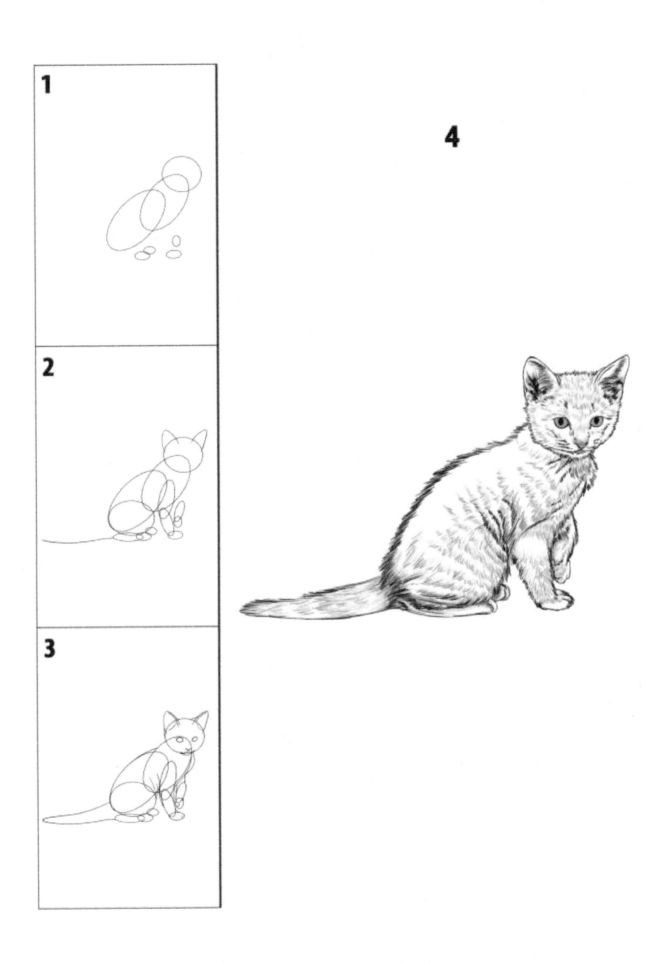

Your turn

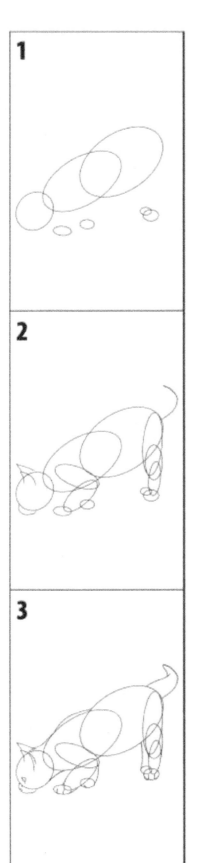

4

Your turn

GOOD JOB!!!

CONCLUSION

THANK YOU SO MUCH FOR PURCHASING THIS BOOK. IF YOU ENJOYED IT, THEN PLEASE LEAVE AN AMAZON REVIEW. REVIEWS ARE THE LIVELIHOOD OF OUR PUBLISHING ENDEAVORS. LEAVING A POSITIVE REVIEW WOULD MEAN THE WORLD TO US.

Made in the USA
Coppell, TX
09 December 2024

42133013R00037